Liberty Bell

A Buddy Book
by
Julie Murray

ABDO
Publishing Company

VISIT US AT
www.abdopub.com

Published by ABDO Publishing Company, 4940 Viking Drive, Edina, Minnesota 55435.

Copyright © 2005 by Abdo Consulting Group, Inc. International copyrights reserved in all countries. No part of this book may be reproduced in any form without written permission from the publisher. Buddy Books™ is a trademark and logo of ABDO Publishing Company.

Printed in the United States.

Edited by: Christy DeVillier
Contributing Editors: Michael P. Goecke, Sarah Tieck
Graphic Design: Deborah Coldiron
Image Research: Deborah Coldiron
Photographs: Comstock, Getty Images, Hulton Archives, Library of Congress, Photodisc

Library of Congress Cataloging-in-Publication Data

Murray, Julie, 1969-
  Liberty Bell / Julie Murray.
      p. cm. — (All aboard America)
  Includes index.
  Summary: A brief history of the Liberty Bell and how it came to symbolize freedom to Americans.
  ISBN 1-59197-507-7
      1. Liberty Bell—Juvenile literature. 2. Philadelphia (Pa.)—Buildings, structures,
    etc.—Juvenile literature. [1. Liberty Bell. 2. Philadelphia (Pa.)—Buildings, structures, etc.]
    I. Title.

F158.8.I3M87 2003
974.8'11—dc21
                                                        2003050309

Table of Contents

Symbol of Freedom

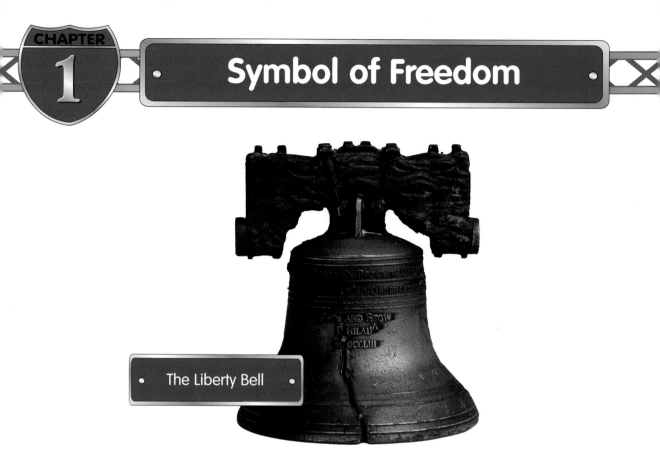

The Liberty Bell

The Liberty Bell is a part of American history. It has rung for many important events. The Liberty Bell is on display in Philadelphia, Pennsylvania. It is famous for its large crack.

The Liberty Bell has a special message on it. It says, "Proclaim Liberty throughout all the land unto all the inhabitants thereof." The word "liberty" means to be free. The Liberty Bell has become a **symbol** of American freedom.

The State House Bell

Congress approves the Declaration of Independence at the Pennsylvania State House.

In 1751, Pennsylvania ordered a bell for their new State House. The State House was a meeting place for Pennsylvania lawmakers. Today, the Pennsylvania State House is called Independence Hall.

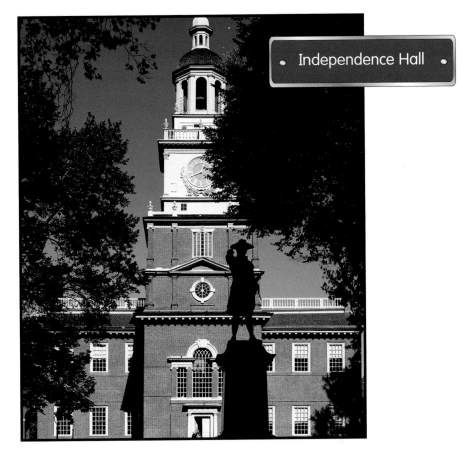

Independence Hall

The State House Bell was made at the Whitechapel Foundry in England. It arrived in Pennsylvania in 1752. People rang the bell to test its sound. Right away, the State House Bell cracked.

Pennsylvania needed a stronger bell. They hired John Pass and John Stow to make one. Pass and Stow broke the old State House Bell into pieces. They melted the pieces and added copper. Pass and Stow believed more copper would make the bell stronger.

Philadelphia tried out the new bell on March 29, 1753. Nobody liked the bell's sound. So, Pass and Stow made another bell. It weighed 2,080 pounds (943 kg). **Citizens** hung the heavy bell in the Pennsylvania State House and rang it. They did not like this bell's sound, either.

Citizens test the sound of Pass and Stow's first bell in 1753.

Pass and Stow's names are on the Liberty Bell.

Pennsylvania ordered a new bell from the Whitechapel Foundry. The new bell did not sound better than Pass and Stow's bell. Pennsylvania kept Pass and Stow's bell hanging in the bell tower. This is the bell that has become the famous Liberty Bell.

Ringing the Liberty Bell brought **citizens** together to hear news. People rang the Liberty Bell for special events, too. It rang in 1761 for the crowning of King George III.

The Liberty Bell also rang for the First Continental Congress. This was a meeting of American leaders at the Pennsylvania State House in 1774.

The **Revolutionary War** began in 1775. In 1776, the Second Continental Congress made plans to break away from Britain. It chose Thomas Jefferson to write America's **Declaration of Independence**. American leaders signed it on July 4, 1776.

July 8, 1776, was an important day in America. The Liberty Bell rang and people gathered at the Pennsylvania State House. Colonel John Nixon read the Declaration of Independence to everyone there.

Hiding The Bell

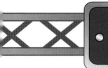

During the **Revolutionary War**, the bell needed to be protected. In the fall of 1777, the British were close to taking over Philadelphia.

Philadelphia **citizens** made plans to hide anything of value. They took down the town's bell. Citizens feared British soldiers would use the bell's metal to make cannons.

Citizens took the Liberty Bell to Allentown, Pennsylvania. They hid it under the floor of Old Zion Reformed Church. The bell stayed hidden there until June 1778.

On October 19, 1781, the British Army surrendered in Yorktown, Virginia. The United States won the **Revolutionary War**.

The last battle of the Revolutionary War took place in Yorktown, Virginia.

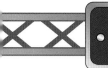

Today the Liberty Bell has a large crack. There are many stories about when the crack appeared.

Some people say the Liberty Bell cracked as it rang for George Washington's birthday. They believe it happened on February 22, 1832. Others say the bell cracked on July 8, 1835. This is the day of Chief Justice John Marshall's funeral.

By 1846, the cracked Liberty Bell's ring sounded odd. People repaired the bell to restore its proper sound. The Liberty Bell rang one last time on George Washington's birthday. February 22, 1846, was the last time people heard its full ring.

George Washington fights in the Revolutionary War.

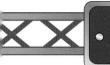

The Liberty Bell was called the State House Bell for many years. Abolitionists were the first people to use "Liberty Bell." Abolitionists are people who fought against slavery. The Liberty Bell became a **symbol** of the anti-slavery movement.

Abolitionists speaking out against slavery.

In 1837, the Anti-Slavery Society printed a booklet. It was called the *Anti-Slavery Record*. In this booklet, the writer talks about Philadelphia's famous bell. This booklet is the first to print the Liberty Bell's new name. Another abolitionist booklet had a poem called "The Liberty Bell."

The United States celebrated its 200th birthday in 1976. That year, Philadelphia's city leaders moved the Liberty Bell. They put it in a glass case at the Liberty Bell Pavilion. This made it easy for people to visit the famous bell.

Philadelphia opened a new pavilion for the Liberty Bell in 2003. It is where the President's House once stood.

The Liberty Bell is famous around the world.

The Liberty Bell is part of Independence Day celebrations today. People softly tap it every Fourth of July. More than one million people visit the Liberty Bell each year. The United States is proud of its famous **symbol** of freedom.

Detour ▼

Did You Know?

- The pitch of the Liberty Bell's ring is an E-flat.
- The Liberty Bell is mostly made of copper and tin.
- The Liberty Bell is about 12 feet (4 m) around at its lip.
- The City of Philadelphia owns the Liberty Bell.
- The Liberty Bell's crack is about 28 inches (71 cm) long.

Important Words

citizen (SI-tih-zun) a member of a city or town.

Declaration of Independence (de-klah-ray-shun uv in-duh-PEN-duns) a very important paper in America's history. It explains that America is ready to rule itself as an independent country.

Revolutionary War (re-vuh-LOO-shuh-nehr-ee WAR) the war Americans fought to win their freedom from Britain.

symbol (SIM-bul) an object or mark that stands for an idea.

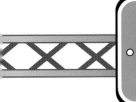

Web Sites

Would you like to learn more
about the Liberty Bell?
Please visit ABDO Publishing Company on the
information superhighway to find Web site links about
the Liberty Bell. These links are routinely
monitored and updated to provide the most current
information available.

www.abdopub.com

YOUR NEXT STOP ABDO PUBLISHING EXIT NOW

Index